THE ROAD TO REVOLUTION

★★★★★★★★★★★★★★★★★★★★★★★★★★★★★★

by Linda Armstrong
illustrated by Corbin Hillam

Author
Linda Armstrong

Illustrator
Corbin Hillam

Cover Illustration and Select Transparencies
Art Kirchhoff

Book Design and Production
Good Neighbor Press, Inc.

TABLE OF CONTENTS ★★★★★★★★★★★★★★★★★★★★★★

Activities marked with an * can be used with one of the transparencies at the back of the book.

Activities

Transparencies

MP4824

In addition to serving as an introduction to the starred activity pages, the transparencies included in this book may be used to assist with displays, research assignments, and other group projects related to the unit.

The Road to Revolution: A Map

Back this transparency with a sheet of white paper to make individual photocopies. Have students keep the map in a project folder and update it as the unit progresses. Project the transparency and use a clear transparency sheet on top so you can add the names of rivers, bays, and mountain ranges without marking on the original. Students may use color to differentiate the colonies on their copies. They may also add the lands of Native American tribes.

The transparency may be projected beside a contemporary map of the United States. Encourage students to compare the present boundaries of the nation with the boundaries on the transparency. Ask them to notice which things have not changed. Ask how geography has affected the work people do, the kinds of houses they live in, and the kinds of recreation they prefer. Have the students write three questions that can be answered by looking at the map, such as "Which colony was farthest south?" or "Which colony was the smallest?" Tell them to include the answers. In another session, shuffle the corrected papers and divide them into two stacks. Divide the class into two teams. Points are scored for correct answers.

The Plymouth Colony

Use this transparency as a starting point for creating a diorama of the settlement at the Plymouth Plantation. This may be done with cardboard, light wood, or even clay, depending on the scale. Divide the class into committees. Each group will pretend to be in charge of a separate aspect of life at Plymouth. Ideas for committees include: religion, entertainment and play, schooling, clothing, food, furniture, houses, kitchen gardens, fields, relationships with the Native Americans, medicine, trade with the outside world, and transportation.

Individual students may talk about the trip over on the Mayflower, experiences with the leaky Speedwell, or the writing and signing of the Mayflower Compact.

Help students write and produce a play about the arrival of the Pilgrims from the point of view of the Wampanoag Indians. Create a mural of a Wampanoag village to use as a set for this play or construct a Wampanoag home based on this transparency and pictures from other sources. The play could include an argument between some members of the tribe who want to attack the Pilgrims and others who feel sorry for them and want to help.

A Hornbook

This transparency may be used as the starting place for a study of early schools. After reading about colonial schools in other sources, help the entire class participate in a reenactment of a day at a colonial school. Have them make dunce caps and make a list of offenses that might be punished by wearing them. Help them discuss the reasons such punishments worked and the reasons they are not still used. Have them invent reading lessons that might have been used with a hornbook. Start a list on the bulletin board of books that were available to people before 1700. Talk about newspapers and other ways people got news. Discuss colonial printing methods. Help students make printing blocks using art gum erasers or potatoes. Have them use stamp pads to print their blocks. Discuss the advantages and disadvantages of teaching all citizens to read. Later, around the time of the Civil War, it was against the law to teach slaves to read in some places. Ask students why anyone would pass such a law.

Many colonists took great pride in their handwriting. They used fine letters on gravestones, signed items they made and crafted samplers. Have the students practice writing a few sentences in colonial script. Ask them to look in books, magazines and on the computer to find at least 5 different alphabets in use today. Help them write the letter R in each of those alphabets.

The Boston Tea Party

This transparency may be used as a starting place to talk about the differences between ships that carry freight now and the ships that carried goods in 1775. Help students use other sources to find out how long the trip from London to Boston Harbor took around 1775. Help them find out how long it takes a ship to make the same trip today. Ask why trade and taxes on traded items were important to both the British and the Americans. Ask what a harbor is and why it is important.

Help students find out what climate is needed to grow tea. Help them find out where tea was grown and prepared for market. Ask how the tea trade affected China. Ask students what hot drink many colonists

MP4824

chose during the Revolutionary War and continued to drink afterward (instead of tea).

Have students make a chart of all the taxes the British imposed on the colonists in the 1770s as they tried to pay back some of their war debts. On the chart include the way each tax was to be collected (a stamp, etc.). Help the students list the taxes their parents pay today. Ask why governments have taxes. Discuss the advantages and disadvantages of each type of tax.

Have the students project the transparency onto a large sheet of paper and paint a stage set for the play which they will write on the activity sheet. Videotape the plays and show the tape at a Parent Night event or take still pictures with a digital camera and print them, with student narration, in staple-bound or hand-stitched books.

The Regulars Are Coming!

This transparency may be used to create a set for dramatic readings of Longfellow's "Paul Revere's Ride." Have students write poems or stories about other people who either rode or participated that night. One could be the guard at the house where Sam Adams and John Hancock were staying. Another could be Dawes, who also rode to warn the patriots, taking a different route. Other possibilities include the men who rowed Paul Revere across the Charles River, the man who provided the horse, the men who put the signal lights in the tower of Old North Church, a farmer or inn-keeper who heard Revere's message, and the British soldiers who stopped the riders outside Lexington.

Help the students find out why the British were marching to Concord and why they wanted to capture Sam Adams and John Hancock. Act out scenes from Longfellow's poem.

Have the students write a short poem using Longfellow's pattern of rhyme and meter in "Paul Revere's Ride.

Discuss ways news traveled in colonial days. Ask students to list the ways people get important personal and national news today.

Revolutionary Flags

Use this transparency as a starting place for research on other flags used during the Revolutionary War. Divide the class into groups. Have each group research one flag. Have them find out where the flag was flown and what the symbols meant. Have them make a small

version of the flag for the map on the bulletin board. Have each group create a large flag on tag board with either tempera paint or glue and colored paper. Display the flags around the room or in the hall. Have each group create a caption for the flag. Help the students create a classroom book about the flags of the Revolutionary War.

The Revolutionary War at Sea

This transparency will help students understand how sea battles were fought in the late 1770s. Encourage the students to find out more about John Paul Jones. Ask them why it was important to capture British merchant ships. Help the students use other reference sources to find out more about the original submarine, The Turtle. Ask them who invented it, how it worked and why it failed to sink the British ship.

Have the students create a chart of different types of sailing ships in use at the time of the Revolutionary War. Help them notice similarities and differences among them.

The most famous paintings of American naval battles were done later from descriptions. Have the students look up some famous American painters of the Revolutionary period. Have a classroom display of prints of early American paintings. Many of the early American artists were limners, or portrait painters. There were no cameras, so people had pictures painted of their relatives so they could remember what they looked like. Have the students draw each other.

Uniforms and Weapons

This transparency will help students see that there was more than one uniform for each side. Have students use other sources to find as many different uniforms for each side as they can. Have them trace the soldiers from the transparency and then dress them in the different uniforms. Pictures may be colored with marker, colored pencil or crayon, depending on the paper. French and Hessian uniforms should be included.

Break the class up into groups. Have each group research a different battle in the Revolutionary War. Help the groups create presentations using slides, transparencies, posters, or drama to bring the battles to life. Each group report should include the reason for the battle, who fought, who the leaders were, the types of weapons used and other equipment.

MP4824

TIMELINE OF THE COLONIES AND REVOLUTION

Between 1600 and 1782	Dutch and Swedish colonists create settlements along the East Coast. The French settle in Canada and claim the watershed of the Mississippi. The Spanish control Florida, settle Santa Fe in New Mexico, and establish missions in California.
1607	English colonists found Jamestown.
1619	Virginia colonists create the House of Burgesses.
1619	Captured Africans arrive at Jamestown.
1620–21	Pilgrims found Plymouth Colony.
1630s	The first colonial public school opens in Boston.
1636–37	Roger Williams and Anne Hutchison establish communities in Rhode Island.
1675–76	The Wampanoags fight the settlers in King Philip's War.
1689–1763	In a series of wars, France and Great Britain fight for control of North America. Britain wins.
1763–74	To cover war debts and limit expansion, Britain imposes new taxes and rules on the colonists.
1773	Colonists hold the Boston Tea Party to protest the new taxes.
1775	Paul Revere rouses the countryside. Patriots meet the Redcoats at Lexington and Concord. The Revolutionary War begins.
1776	Thomas Paine's pamphlet, *Common Sense*, lists reasons for separating from Britain.
1776	Thomas Jefferson writes the *Declaration of Independence*. It is adopted in Philadelphia on July 4.
1776	Before he is executed for spying on the British, the young scholar and athlete Nathan Hale declares, "I only regret that I have but one life to give for my country."
1777	When Americans defeat the British at Saratoga, France decides to support the Patriots.
1779	John Paul Jones, daring captain of the *Bonhomme Richard*, captures the British warship *Serapis* in the English Channel.
1781	The British surrender at Yorktown. Plans for a new government, the *Articles of Confederation*, are adopted.
1787	A better plan for government, the *Constitution*, is written.
1789	George Washington becomes the first President of the United States.
1791	James Madison writes the *Bill of Rights*, 10 amendments to the *Constitution* which protect the rights of individual citizens.

Copyright © 2003 Milliken Publishing Co.
MP4824

The First European Settlements ☆★☆★☆★☆★☆★☆★☆

Early European visitors to the East Coast of what is now the United States returned home with tales of rich fishing grounds, fine farmland, and tall forests filled with game. In crowded Old World countries, rich people owned the best land. Big farms were handed down from father to son. Many people had to work for these landowners. In the New World there seemed to be land for anyone with the courage to take it. Many were ready to try.

Life in the wilderness proved to be much harder than the first adventurers expected. Many died of starvation. Smallpox, scurvy, and pneumonia killed others. The lucky ones went home on supply ships.

In spite of nightmarish stories, hopeful people continued to board ships bound for new colonies. Finally, a few settlements survived. Among them were Jamestown, St. Augustine, and Quebec.

These first successful English, French, and Spanish settlers learned how to handle the dangers of the new land. As sources of emergency food and supplies, established towns helped later colonies survive.

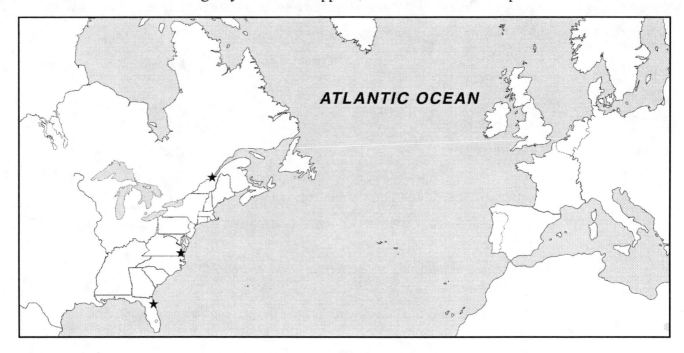

ATLANTIC OCEAN

1. Color France yellow. Color England red. Color Spain orange. Color Holland green.

2. Label Jamestown, St. Augustine, and Quebec. Use other sources to find out what country settled each town.

Jamestown: _____ St. Augustine: _____

Quebec: _____

Did You Know?
Captured Native Americans were prized in Europe
as sources of information about the New World.

★☆★☆★☆★☆★☆★☆★☆★☆★☆★☆★☆★☆★☆★☆★☆

MP4824

ENGLISH, DUTCH, SWEDISH, SPANISH, AND FRENCH ☆★☆★☆

By 1640 many European countries had settlements in North America. The British claimed most of the land along the eastern coast of what is now the United States. Holland claimed the area between the Delaware River and the Connecticut River and purchased Manhattan Island from the Native Americans. Swedish settlers moved into a small piece of land on the Delaware. The French settled in what is now Canada, with a center in Quebec. The Spanish claimed Florida. They also had settlements and claims in the Southwest.

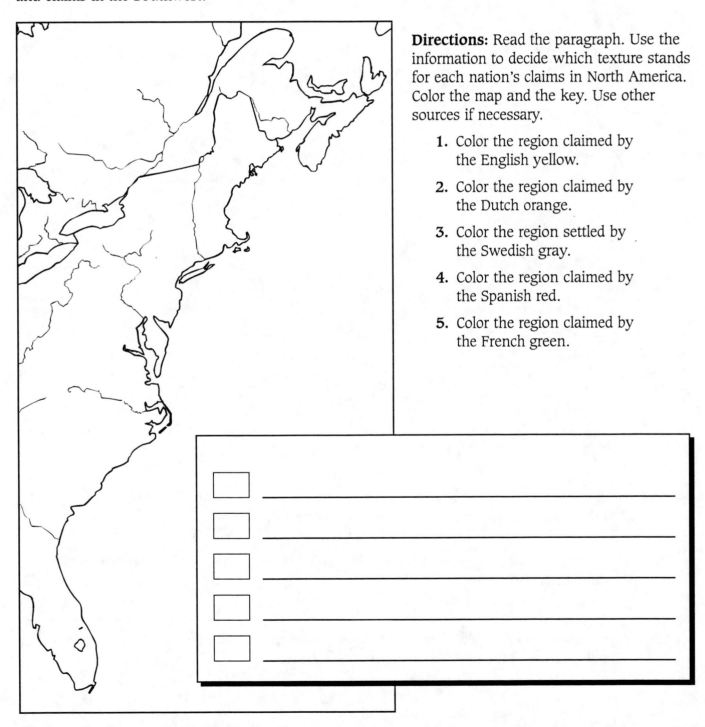

Directions: Read the paragraph. Use the information to decide which texture stands for each nation's claims in North America. Color the map and the key. Use other sources if necessary.

1. Color the region claimed by the English yellow.

2. Color the region claimed by the Dutch orange.

3. Color the region settled by the Swedish gray.

4. Color the region claimed by the Spanish red.

5. Color the region claimed by the French green.

WHOSE LAND IS THIS ANYWAY? ★★★★★★★★★★★★★★

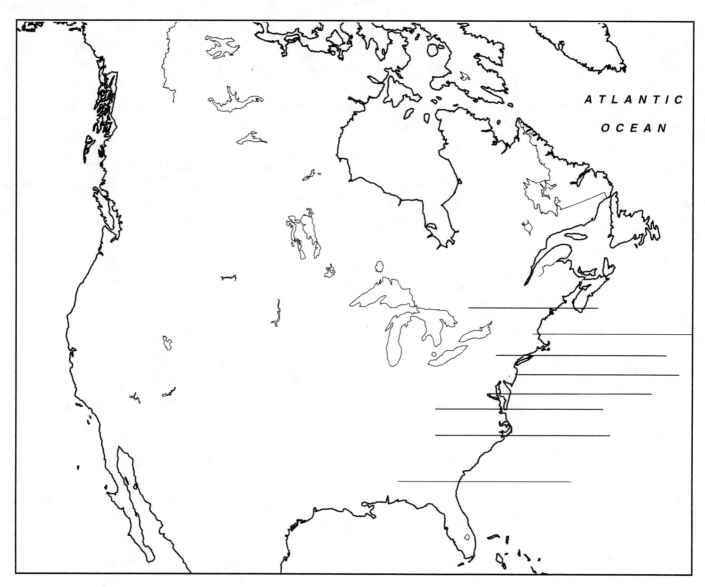

ATLANTIC

OCEAN

1. Use the transparency or other sources to write the names of the following Native American tribes in their home territories on the map: A. Iroquois B. Delaware C. Cherokee D. Creek E. Shawnee F. Hurons G.Powhatan H.Wampanoag.

2. Draw pictures of the two kinds of homes the Wampanoags lived in before the Pilgrims arrived. What are those houses made of?

_____

3. In other reference sources find out what kinds of houses the Cherokee and Iroquois tribes lived in. Draw pictures of their homes on another paper.

4 ★★★★★★★★★★★★★★★★★★★★★★★★★★★★★★★★

Courage, Hope, and a Very Leaky Ship ☆★☆★☆★☆★☆

One very famous group of settlers came to the New World in November of 1620. They did not build the first successful British colony. That honor belonged to Jamestown, a settlement developed by hardy, adventurous men. The Pilgrims created a real town that included families.

At first, their trip seemed doomed. One of the ships they planned to use, the Speedwell, was so leaky that it had to be left behind. Some of the Pilgrims stayed behind and the rest crowded into the Mayflower, a merchant ship that had once hauled tar, lumber, fish, spices, and wine. When the settlers finally reached land, it was Cape Cod, far north of the Virginia plot they had planned to settle.

In spite of their troubles, they did not give up. They wanted to create a colony where they would be free to practice their religion. They waited out the long cold winter on the ship and in the spring they started to build.

Look at the cross section and read the paragraph above. Answer the questions true or false.

1. The Poop Deck is at the bottom of the hold. _____

2. The Bowsprit is on the front of the ship. _____

3. The Main mast is a room for storing food. _____

4. The hold is a place below decks for storing supplies. _____

5. The Pilgrims landed in the wrong place. _____

6. Jamestown was the first successful British settlement. _____

7. The Pilgrims celebrated Thanksgiving as soon as they landed. _____

8. The Pilgrims came to America to make money. _____

9. The Mayflower's crew slept in the back part of the ship. _____

10. The Mayflower had always been a passenger ship. _____

Did You Know?

There was more than one Mayflower. It was a common name for ships.

★☆★☆★☆★☆★☆★☆★☆★☆★☆★☆★☆★☆★☆★☆★☆★☆★☆★ **5**

MP4824

Name ____

THE IMPORTANCE OF THE MAYFLOWER COMPACT ★★★★★

The Pilgrims came from a country where kings or queens made most of the rules. When they left for the New World, the Pilgrims had a charter to develop a private plantation within the Virginia Colony. As it turned out, the Mayflower did not land in Virginia. It was blown off course and ended up in Massachusetts.

The Pilgrims did not have a charter for the land on Cape Cod. That meant they had no official government. According to an account by William Bradford, some of the colonists who were not Pilgrims started talking about using "their owne libertie."

The Pilgrims understood that to survive, everyone would have to work together. Before landing the ship, the passengers decided to write an agreement that would allow the community to elect leaders and create rules.

The document they wrote, the Mayflower Compact, was meant to be temporary, but when people outside of the Mayflower heard about it, they started thinking. Was it really possible for people to live without kings and queens? Could they make decisions by discussing issues and voting? A hundred and fifty years later, Patriots answered that question with a resounding yes.

Directions: Look up the Mayflower Compact in another reference source. Have a class discussion about what kinds of rules your school must have to do its job. If your class were in charge of the whole school, how would you make rules to keep it working well? How would you decide the punishments for rule-breakers? Write a Compact for your class.

____

____

____

____

____

____

____

____

____

____

(continue on another paper)

WILD RIVERS, DENSE FORESTS AND RICH FIELDS ★★★★★

The original 13 colonies fell into three groups; New England, the Middle Colonies, and the Southern Colonies.

Cold in winter and strewn with rocks left behind by retreating glaciers, New England was not an easy land for farmers, but its harbors were good and the Atlantic just off its shores teemed with fish. The great forests that crowded in around settlements provided raw materials for ship building and barrel making, occupations which supplied great natural ports such as Boston Harbor. Farms in New England tended to be small and their owners were more concerned with supporting their families than making money.

The Middle Colonies had good ports, good fishing, and easily plowed sandy soils. Colonists there grew wheat and other grains. Iron, textile, and paper mills developed Maryland and Pennsylvania.

The Southern Colonies had the hottest summers, the mildest winters, and the richest farmland. Tobacco, rice, and indigo grew well there. Tobacco was hard to grow. It wore out the land and took a lot of workers. Large farms became the centers of life and culture. Because plantations needed cheap labor, it was not long before slavery became an important part of the economy in the Southern Colonies.

1. Label the Mississippi, Ohio, St. Lawrence, and Delaware Rivers.

2. Label Chesapeake Bay, Boston Harbor, Hudson Bay, and Charleston Harbor.

3. Label the Allegheny Mountains, the Appalachian Mountains, and the Catskills.

4. Use other sources to find the average January and July temperatures in

   Boston, Massachusetts _____,

   Philadelphia, Pennsylvania _____, and

   Atlanta, Georgia _____.

5. Color the New England colonies red, the Middle Colonies green, and the Southern Colonies orange.

★☆★☆★☆★☆★☆★☆★☆★☆★☆★☆★☆★☆★☆★☆★☆★ **7**

MP4824

Name _____

DIFFERENT COLONIES FOR DIFFERENT REASONS ★☆★☆★☆

Each of the thirteen original colonies was started for a different reason.

Use other sources to help you match each colony with an interesting fact about its origins. Write the correct letter in each blank.

1. Virginia _____
2. Massachusetts _____
3. South Carolina _____
4. Georgia _____
5. New York _____
6. Pennsylvania _____
7. New Jersey _____
8. Delaware _____
9. Rhode Island _____
10. Connecticut _____
11. Maryland _____
12. North Carolina _____
13. New Hampshire _____

a. refuge for English Catholics
b. last colony established
c. Where the Pilgrims landed
d. money-maker for friends of Charles II
e. first successful British colony
f. Site of Roanoke Island
g. Separated from Massachusetts in 1679
h. Once settled by the Dutch
i. Named after William Penn
j. Once settled by Sweden
k. Formed by Pilgrims banished from their colony for being too liberal.
l. Once divided into East and West sections, but reunited.
m. wanted stricter rules than the Pilgrims

14. Label the 13 original colonies on the map.

Name _____

Daily Life in the Colonies ★★★★★★★★★★★★★★★★★★

Directions: Use reference sources to find out what a colonial house looked like inside. Draw a "Keeping Room" or main room. Include and label each of the following: the source of heat, a place to sit, a place to hang clothes, children's toys, a sampler, a place to store food, a way to make cloth or clothes.

Use other sources to find the meaning of each word. Write it on the line.

1. trundle bed _____

2. pung _____

3. town crier _____

4. cobbler _____

5. blacksmith _____

6. tanner _____

7. wag-on-the-wall _____

8. cooper _____

9. whitesmith _____

10. post rider _____

★★★★★★★★★★★★★★★★★★★★★★★★★★★★★ **9**

MP4824

Make a Hornbook ★★★★★★★★★★★★★★★★★★★★★★★

Colonial children did not have reading books. They learned to read from a page with letters and numbers. Paper was very expensive, so this page had to be used over and over. It was mounted on a wooden paddle to make it easy to carry. Because it was protected by a piece of transparent animal horn, it was called a hornbook.

To make a hornbook of your own you will need scissors, a cereal box, brown construction paper, white multipurpose paper, paste or glue, a black watercolor marker, tape, clear plastic and a stapler.

1. Cut out both large sides of the box.

2. Trace the paddle shape on this page onto each piece of cardboard and cut the pieces out.

3. Cut sheets of brown construction paper to fit the paddles. Use a dark marker to add a wood grain if you wish. Glue one piece of construction paper to each piece of cardboard. Let it dry.

4. Trace the "page" shape onto white paper. Cut it out and glue it in the center of one of the "paddle" shapes.

5. With the marker, write the letters of the alphabet and the numerals from 0 to 9. Use colonial letters. Notice how their printing was the same as ours and how it was different.

6. Place the two paddles back to back and staple along the edges. Cover the white paper with plastic and staple it in place.

★★★★★★★★★★★★★★★★★★★★★★★★★★★★

MP4824

TOAD TEA AND RATTLESNAKE OIL ★★★★★★★★★★★★★★★

Doctors, surgeons and apothecaries, or pharmacists, came to the colonies from England. The doctors studied in universities, just as doctors do today. A few of their treatments are still used. Surgeons learned their craft as apprentices. They knew anatomy and could perform operations, but they did not know about germs. Infections often killed their patients. Apothecaries made medicines from different chemicals and herbs.

In America these specialists tried to practice medicine as they had in England, but they soon found out it did not work. The settlements were too small and far apart to support three different professionals. Each doctor had to learn to do his own surgery and make his own medicines.

Doctors traveled great distances on horseback or in wagons, so it took them a long time to reach people who were sick. Doctors were also very expensive. People soon learned how to treat diseases and injuries at home. They grew special plants called "herbs" in their kitchen gardens. They boiled the herbs in water to make teas or they ground them up and mixed them with honey to make syrups.

Some of their prescriptions were strange. For example, one treatment called for a tea made of toads which had been roasted and then ground into a powder. If a baby cried because his teeth were coming in, a colonial mother might have hung a necklace made of wolf teeth around his neck. Rattlesnake oil was used for many problems.

In colonial times, people often recovered from injuries and illnesses by staying warm and comfortable in bed. Doctors still tell us to get plenty of rest when we are sick.

There were some very effective medicines in colonial times. In the early 1700s, for example, doctors started using a vaccine against smallpox, a disease which had killed many people in Europe and America.

1. Name three ways colonial doctors were the same and three ways they were different from doctors today?

   _____

2. Name some ways people treated diseases and injuries in colonial times.

   _____

3. Three types of doctors came to the colonies from England. Name them.

   _____

4. Why did many people treat illnesses and injuries at home?

   _____

5. Name one thing doctors know now that colonial doctors did not know.

   _____

6. Name some diseases doctors still do not know how to cure.

   _____

★★★★★★★★★★★★★★★★★★★★★★★★★★★★★★★★★★★★★★ 11

 MP4824

MAKE A CORN HUSK DOLL ★☆★☆★☆★☆★☆★☆★☆★☆★☆★☆★☆

Children in colonial times could not visit the mall, but they did have toys. Tops and marbles were popular. Native Americans taught the colonists how to make dolls from corn husks.

You can make a corn husk doll of your own. You will need about seven dried corn husks from the produce section of your local market, a ball of twine, a bowl of water and a pair of scissors.

1. Soak the husks to soften them.

2. Lay four husks together.

3. Tie them together.

4. Fold husk bottoms down over the tied edges to form the head.

5. Tie the neck.

6. Roll another husk to form the arms.

7. Slide the arms between the layers of husks.

8. Tie the waist.

9. Tie four husks to the bottom.

10. Leave them loose as a skirt or separate them into two legs. Add ties for knees and ankles. Add features with a marking pen.

MP4824

Name _____

Come to Our Tea Party! ★☆★★☆★★☆★★☆★★☆★★☆★★☆

It is early in the evening of December 16, 1773. You are a Patriot named John. You are a tailor by trade and you live in Boston. Usually you wear fine clothes, but tonight you are dressed as a Native American. Your face is smeared with paint. Most people would not recognize you.

A British ship filled with tea for the people of the Colonies has sailed into the harbor. You are on your way to meet other Patriots. Your mission is to protest Britain's high taxes by sneaking aboard the ship and dumping that tea into the ocean.

You stop by a friend's house. His name is Tom. You talk him into coming with you to the Boston Tea Party. John will tell you why he doesn't want to go. Your arguments must convince him. Write this as a play.

John: _____

Tom: _____

John: _____

Tom: _____

John: _____

Tom: _____

John: _____

Tom: _____

John: _____

Tom: _____

Action? _____

★☆★☆★☆★☆★☆★☆★☆★☆★☆★☆★☆★☆★☆★☆★☆★☆★☆★☆★☆★ **13**

                                                                 MP4824

Name _____

How a Poet Created a Hero ★☆★★★☆★★★☆★★★☆

In 1863, when the United States was in the middle of the Civil War, a former Harvard professor named Henry Wadsworth Longfellow published a book called *The Tales of a Wayside Inn*. The first poem in that book made history. It was "Paul Revere's Ride." It became so popular that many people forgot it was just a story based, loosely, on facts. They believed every detail.

Longfellow's grandfather had worked with George Washington. His father had been a friend of Lafayette, a French aristocrat who helped the colonial army during the Revolutionary War. In the 1860s Longfellow was America's most popular poet. He wanted to do something to help his country. Longfellow wanted to show people that with courage they could help their country survive hard times.

Paul Revere was a true hero in the Revolution. He and his friends watched the British troops. There were no telephones. There was no Internet. Messengers on horseback like Revere helped Patriots keep in touch with each other. In the middle of April of 1775 British actions showed that they were getting ready to march up Lexington Road to arrest Sam Adams and John Hancock. They were also going to destroy a stash of weapons and ammunition stored at Concord. They wanted to do this quickly and secretly.

Paul Revere and other riders, including William Dawes and Samuel Prescott, warned the Patriots, who were ready to fight when the Regulars, or British soldiers, arrived.

1. Read the poem "Paul Revere's Ride." Choose one or two friends. Take turns reading stanzas. Choose parts of the poem to read together. Longfellow tried to make the rhythm of the poem match the sound of a galloping horse. Choose someone in your group to make the sound of a horse galloping. Record your version of the poem on tape.

2. Read Paul Revere's version of his ride or another factual account in a history book. On another paper, make a chart comparing the events in the poem to the actual events. Include columns for information that is the same and for information that is different.

3. Discuss current movies(stories, not documentaries)about things that have happened in history. Do you think everything in those movies is true? Why or why not?

4. Why is Paul Revere more famous than the other men who rode out that night to warn the Patriots that the Regulars were on their way to Concord?

14 ★★★☆★★☆★★☆★★☆★★☆★★☆★★☆★★☆★★☆★★☆

                                                    MP4824

Colonial and Revolutionary Money ★☆★☆★☆★☆★☆

The British wanted the colonies to make them rich. British merchants sold more things to the colonists than they bought from them. The colonists got money from other countries for the things they made or grew on their plantations. They sent most of this money to England to pay for cloth, tea, and other supplies.

There were not enough English coins for people in the colonies to buy the things they needed from each other. Sometimes the colonists paid for things with coins from Holland and France. The most common coins were high-quality silver dollars from Spain and Latin America. The sizes of current U.S. coins are based on Spanish, not English, money.

Often, goods were used instead of money. A doctor or school master might be paid in tobacco leaves. A farmer might send wheat to England to pay for needed supplies. This was known as "commodity money." Sometimes Native American wampum, or shell money, was used for small change.

The Patriot hero, Paul Revere, had an important job. He made vases and tableware out of silver. Many people had silver items. They were like money in the bank. Silver always had value. In an emergency, the owner of a silver spoon could melt it down and create a coin or two.

During the American Revolution the Continental Congress decided to print paper money, or notes, to pay for the things the army needed. The bills were called "Continentals." By 1779, they were worthless. They were like checks written on an account that everyone knew was empty.

Directions:

1. Pretend that your class is a new country. On another paper, design coins and bills. How many different kinds of coins and bills will you need?

2. Why is it bad to have too few different denominations (such as pennies, nickels, and dimes)?

_____

3. Why is it bad to have too many? _____

★☆★☆★☆★☆★☆★☆★☆★☆★☆★☆★☆★☆★☆★☆★☆★☆★ **15**

MP4824

FLAGS OF THE REVOLUTION ★☆★☆★☆★☆★☆★☆★☆★☆★☆

Directions: Use other sources to find the correct colors for each of these flags. Color them. Imagine that your class is a new country. Design a flag for your class. On another paper, write a paragraph about your flag. Explain what each symbol and color stands for.

MP4824

REVOLUTIONARY NEWS

Our motto: If it's not more than 250 years old, it's too new for our news.

REWARD	NOTICE
For the return of one brown horse, stolen by the British in the early hours of April 19. Return to P. Revere, Silversmith.	Wagons will collect pewter bowls, dishes, and other items Tuesday next. Be generous. Our fighting men need bullets!

1. Write a headline in six words or less for each event.
Paul Revere rides to warn the Patriots that the British Regulars are on their way to capture the ammunition hidden at Concord, Massachusetts.

_____

With about 2,400 men, George Washington crosses the icy Delaware River on Christmas night, 1776. They attack the British forces at Trenton, New Jersey. More than 900 Hessian prisoners are captured.

_____

2. Complete the want ads in your own words.

Soldiers Needed for Continental Army	Wanted
No Experience Necessary. Will Train. Benefits include . . . Duties include . . . To apply . . .	Volunteers to make clothes for Continental Soldiers. Should be able to . . . Benefits include . . . Meet at . . .

_____ **Apprentices Needed**

Duties include . . .

Benefits include . . .

To apply . . .

17

Name _____

Paint a Battle at Sea ★★★★★★★★★★★★★★★★★★★★☆

The British Navy at the time of the Revolution was one of the most powerful in the world. British ships attacked ships from other countries that tried to bring supplies to the Americans. An experienced sea captain named John Paul Jones volunteered to help.

When the French joined America in the fight, they let John Paul Jones use their ports. They even gave him a bigger ship. It was called the *Duras*, but Jones renamed it the *Bonhomme Richard* or "Poor Richard" after Benjamin Franklin's famous *Almanack*.

Captain Jones trained his 374 crewmen carefully. In August of 1779 the Bonhomme Richard and some smaller ships sailed up the coast of Scotland and Ireland. On the way back to France they met some British ships that were carrying goods for English businessmen. Two large warships from the British Navy protected them.

One of the warships, the *Serapis*, challenged John Paul Jones to fight. Even though the *Bonhomme Richard* was an older ship and did not have as many guns, John Paul Jones accepted. The two ships drew up side by side and started firing. People watched the battle from the shore of England. It went on into the night.

Jones knew he did not have much time. His ship was starting to sink. He and his men had to capture the *Serapis*. He rammed the back of the bigger ship and, using grappling hooks, his men started to climb aboard, but the British sailors fired muskets at them and many were killed.

The British captain called, "Do you wish to surrender?"

John Paul Jones answered, "I have not yet begun to fight!"

They fought for two hours more. Finally a cannonball from the *Bonhomme Richard* knocked down the mainmast of the *Serapis*, and Jones's men boarded the British ship. The *Bonhomme Richard* sank, but John Paul Jones and his crew had captured the proud *Serapis*.

Back in America, there were celebrations in the streets. Jones's victory showed the people of the United States that, even though it seemed impossible, they could win against England.

Directions: Before cameras or movies were invented, every king and queen paid artists to record important events.

Pretend you are one of these artists. On a sheet of watercolor paper, create a painting of a battle at sea. Sketch the ships, the horizon, and clouds before you begin to paint. Most battle paintings in Revolutionary times were done with oil paints on stretched canvas panels. You will use tempera paints, crayons, or watercolors.

18 ★★★★★★★★★★★★★★★★★★★★★★★★★★★☆

Name _____

FIGHTING WORDS ★☆★☆★☆★☆★☆★☆★☆★☆★☆★☆★☆★☆★☆

Directions: Use other sources to find the meaning of each of these "fighting words." Mark the circle in front of the correct choice. On another paper, draw pictures to illustrate two of these words.

1. hatchet
   ○ an early hand gun
   ○ an ax
   ○ a hat

2. spontoon
   ○ a pole weapon
   ○ a bowl for spit
   ○ a kind of boot

3. breeches
   ○ cannons on ships
   ○ dried rations
   ○ pants

4. musket
   ○ a furry animal that hung around
      camps
   ○ a gun
   ○ a boat

5. frontier hunting shirt
   ○ a British spy uniform
   ○ a uniform for Continentals
   ○ worn in frontier battles only

6. dragoon
   ○ a foot soldier
   ○ a soldier on horseback
   ○ an early tank

7. powder horn
   ○ a present for ladies at home
   ○ a musical instrument played in battle
   ○ a container for gun powder

8. haversack
   ○ a large gun
   ○ a gun cart
   ○ a soldier's linen satchel

9. cannon
   ○ a field gun
   ○ a container
   ○ shoes

10. fife
    ○ shoulder decorations on a uniform
    ○ a musical instrument
    ○ a tent

11. tricorn
    ○ rations
    ○ a tent
    ○ a hat

12. bicorn
    ○ a hat
    ○ a two-edged sword
    ○ a battlefield painting

13. Grenadier
    ○ a uniform jacket
    ○ a discharged soldier
    ○ a member of an elite guard

14. indigo
    ○ a blue dye
    ○ a dessert
    ○ a battlefield

15. militia
    ○ a professional army
    ○ citizen soldiers
    ○ the French Navy

16. ammunition
    ○ bullets and shot
    ○ food
    ○ uniforms

17. infantry
    ○ new recruits
    ○ foot soldiers
    ○ very young soldiers

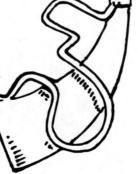

★☆★☆★☆★☆★☆★☆★☆★☆★☆★☆★☆★☆★☆★☆★☆★☆ **19**

MP4824

Name _____

SOME AMAZING PEOPLE ★★★★★★★★★★★★★★★★★★★★

Use reference sources to match the names of these amazing people with their descriptions

Patrick Henry	Benedict Arnold	Paul Revere	Cornwallis
Benjamin Franklin	Nathan Hale	Rochambeau	Lafayette
George Washington	John Hancock	Baron Von Steuben	Thomas Paine

Name   **Description**

1. _____   the first President of the United States

2. _____   a young scholar who was executed for spying on the British

3. _____   a Patriot leader who changed sides and started to help the British

4. _____   a Prussian who helped train Patriot soldiers

5. _____   a Patriot famous for his signature

6. _____   a Patriot who made a famous midnight ride

7. _____   author of the pamphlet "Common Sense"

8. _____   a Patriot said "Give me liberty or give me death!"

9. _____   the British general who surrendered at Yorktown

10. _____   a printer, author, and Patriot who went to France to ask for help

11. _____   a French commander whose well-trained troops helped defeat
Cornwallis at Yorktown

12. _____   a French nobleman who joined the Continental Army at the age
of 19 and became a close friend of George Washington

★★★★★★★★★★★★★★★★★★★★★★★★★★★
MP4824

WRITE A "DECLARATION OF INDEPENDENCE" ★☆★☆★☆★☆

In the spring of 1776 the Second Continental Congress gathered in Philadelphia. American militiamen were already fighting the British. Many delegates to the Continental Congress believed it was time to tell Britain that the colonies wanted to be an independent country. Thomas Jefferson was given the job of writing a draft of the paper that would be sent to the King.

Pretend that you were given Jefferson's job. Write a "Declaration of Independence." Explain why you think the colonies should be independent. Compare your paper with the actual *Declaration of Independence*. How is it the same? How is it different?

MP4824

THE WORLD TURNED UPSIDE DOWN ☆★☆★☆★☆★☆★☆★☆

By the summer of 1781 Washington's bedraggled Continental Army faced its sixth year of fighting. They had won amazing victories and suffered terrible hardships. When the French had joined the American cause in 1778, they had been filled with new hope, but the war had dragged on.

On July 6 Count Jean-Baptiste de Rochambeau marched his army of 5000 well-equipped, well-trained men into Washington's camp in New York. It was a miracle. At first Washington wanted to use the fresh troops to capture New York City, but they would need naval support to do that.

The French admiral de Grasse said he was going to take his ships south to Chesapeake Bay instead. Washington was disappointed, but he changed his plans to take advantage of the situation. He found out that the British general, Cornwallis, was camped with his army in Yorktown on the southern coast.

There was a good chance that the combined Continental and French forces could surround and defeat him. That is exactly what happened. At the beginning of October Washington and his allies started preparing to move in on the little town. The battle was long and furious, with cannons roaring and muskets firing.

Finally, at about nine in the morning on October 17 a British drummer boy climbed up to the top of a pile of rubble and played the drum roll that meant Cornwallis was ready to have a conference. He wanted to surrender.

At that time Great Britain was one of the most powerful nations in the world. The United States was hardly a nation at all. For the Americans to capture one of Britain's finest forces was unthinkable. It was the opposite of everything that seemed logical. It was the "World Turned Upside Down."

There was, at the time, a song with that title, and, according to legend, that is what the British military band played as the soldiers marched by and laid their weapons in huge heaps before Washington's army.

Write your own version of "The World Turned Upside Down."

Make a list of the most ridiculous things you can imagine. For example, perhaps an ant could beat a tiger in a race. Share your list with the class.

1. _____
2. _____
3. _____
4. _____
5. _____
6. _____
7. _____
8. _____
9. _____
10. _____

Sing songs from the American Revolution such as Yankee Doodle.

MP4824

The British did not sign the official peace treaty until 1783, but the War for Independence was over after the surrender at Yorktown. The colonists now had to face other hard realities. They were deeply in debt and they did not have a real government.

They had a framework for running the new country called the Articles of Confederation. It had been adopted in 1777. Unfortunately, it did not work very well. Most of the power was left in the hands of the individual states. The former colonies could not agree on important issues. Nobody was able to make the decisions that had to be made.

In 1787 leaders began to write a new plan for government, the Constitution. It provided for a solid central government, balanced by three branches: the executive, the legislative and the judicial. In 1791 ten amendments were added to guarantee the rights of individual American citizens. It was ratified, or approved, and the United States, under the leadership of its first president, George Washington, took its place among the nations of the world.

REVIEW

Match.

1. _____ George Washington		**a.** a French nobleman
2. _____ Jamestown		**b.** where the Pilgrims landed
3. _____ July 4, 1776		**c.** an agreement to make rules
4. _____ Boston Tea Party		**d.** grew rice and tobacco
5. _____ Lafayette		**e.** convinced the French to help
6. _____ Massachusetts		**f.** a famous traitor
7. _____ The Mayflower Compact		**g.** trained Continental troops
8. _____ Paul Revere		**h.** a sea captain
9. _____ Southern colonies		**i.** Washington crosses the Delaware
10. _____ John Paul Jones		**j.** first President of the U.S.
11. _____ Benjamin Franklin		**k.** a protest against taxes
12. _____ Benedict Arnold		**l.** Declaration of Independence signed
13. _____ Von Steuben		**m.** watched British and warned Patriots
14. _____ Christmas, 1776		**n.** first successful British settlement

MP4824

EARLY AMERICAN TRIVIA ★☆★☆★☆★☆★☆★☆★☆★☆★☆★☆★☆

Because, at first, Benedict Arnold fought heroically for the Patriot cause, there is a memorial for him at West Point. Because he later betrayed that same cause, there is no name on the plaque.

People from many countries assisted the Patriots during the American Revolution. Marquis de Lafayette from France, Bernardo de Galvez from Spain, Baron Friedrich von Steuben from Prussia, and Casimir Pulaski and Thaddeus Kosciusko from Poland all helped.

The Patriot Captain John Stokes was wounded a total of 23 times at the Waxhaws Massacre. Two different British soldiers tried to kill him. Finally a British sergeant convinced their doctor to bandage his wounds. He lived to become an American federal judge.

A few husbands and wives were on different sides in the Revolutionary War. After the war ended, that anger lived on. One husband was so mad that he did not want to be buried next to his wife. He was afraid that on Judgment Day the dead would rise and he didn't want to see her face.

When Paul Revere got to the inn in Lexington where Samuel Adams and John Hancock were staying, the guard told him to stop making so much noise. "Noise!" cried Revere. "You'll have noise enough before long. The Regulars are coming out!"

When the Revolutionary War began, the colonies were cut off from British mills that provided much of their cloth. A magazine editor called for women and girls to help win the war by spending more time at their spinning wheels.

Patriots in New York pulled down a huge statue of King George. Men and women broke it into small pieces, melted the lead, and poured the metal into bullet molds. They made more than 40,000 musket balls, which they fired at the armies of the king.

The original Purple Heart, a military decoration, was created by George Washington to honor special acts of courage. Only three were awarded. In 1932, on the 200th anniversary of Washington's birth, a new Purple Heart was created to honor soldiers wounded in action.

1. Of the items listed above, which surprises you the most? _____

   Why? _____

   _____

   _____

2. Use the Internet or other reference sources to write two other interesting tidbits of information about the American Revolution.

   _____

   _____

MP4824

Name _____

THEN AND NOW ★☆★☆★☆★☆★☆★☆★☆★☆★☆★☆★☆★☆★☆

Life during the American Revolution was very different from what it is today.
Life during the American Revolution was very similar to life today.

How can both these statements be true?

1. Fill in the chart by making an X in the correct column following each item.

	Then	Now	Both
Many farmers grow corn			
Children keep pets			
Boys become apprentices			
People fish			
People enjoy singing			
People read newspapers			
People travel in cars			
Children play with toys			
Children go to school			
People go to inns to hear news			
Boys play marbles			
People drink toad tea to feel better			
Most letter carriers ride on horseback			
Children learn to read from hornbooks			
People watch television			

2. List 10 other ways that life in Colonial and Revolutionary times was similar to life today.

_____

_____

_____

_____

3. From what you've learned of life during the Revolution, what do you think was most different about life then and life today?

_____

_____

_____

★☆★☆★☆★☆★☆★☆★☆★☆★☆★☆★☆★☆★☆★☆★☆ **25**

MP4824

REVOLUTIONARY PROJECTS ★ ★ ★ ★ ★ ★ ★ ★ ★ ★ ★ ★ ★ ★ ★ ★ ☆

Complete one of these projects. Include maps, illustrations, and other appropriate graphics.

- Design and model an outfit worn by a colonist or Revolutionary soldier. Create a character to go with your clothing. Tell the class about your life as that character and be ready to answer questions.
- Create a book of quotations from the Colonial and Revolutionary periods. Illustrate each one and tell a little bit about the person who said the famous lines. Use Colonial calligraphy to write the title on the cover.
- Create a timeline. Use a different line for the life of each of ten people involved in the Revolutionary War. Place the lines one above the other on a long strip of paper. Choose a measure, such as an inch, for each year. Make a line at the top as your index. Mark off every ten years such as 1680, 1690, 1700. See encyclopedias for examples of timelines like this.
- Create a promotional brochure for people in Britain thinking about settling in one of the colonies. Include a map, drawings, and descriptions of the attractions of that colony. Include information about schools, government, jobs, housing, entertainment and churches.
- Imagine you are a colonist traveling from a country in Europe to one of the 13 colonies. Write a diary. Include the length of the trip, conditions on the ship, what it was like to leave home, and what it was like to arrive in the new settlement.
- Make a videotape of an interview with George Washington, Thomas Jefferson, or Benjamin Franklin.
- Write an article for the "Revolutionary Times" about any Revolutionary battle. Be sure to include who, what, when, where, why, and how.
- Write a series of letters between a Patriot drummer boy and his sister at home in one of the colonies. Choose an actual battle for your drummer boy to see and include accurate historical details. Remember that the boy's sister and the mother will be in danger too.
- Write a play based on the writing and signing of the *Declaration of Independence*. With some friends, present your play for the class. Everyone can participate in the celebration at the end.
- Study *Poor Richard's Almanack* by Benjamin Franklin. Create an almanac for your school year. Include helpful advice, important events, and long-range weather forecasts. (Find the weather information in a current almanac or on the Internet.)

Write a 3- to 5-page report on one of these topics:

Benedict Arnold, First American Traitor
Benjamin Franklin
British Soldiers in the Revolutionary War
Captain John Smith
Colonial Recipes and Remedies
Dutch Settlers in the Americas
French Trappers in the Americas
George Washington
Daring Battles of the American Revolution
Life in Britain at the Time of the Revolution
How the French Helped the Patriot Cause
Jobs in the Colonies
King Philip's War
Mail Service in the Colonies
Massachusetts, Pennsylvania, New York, Georgia, or Rhode Island

Native American Tribes in New England
Pocahontas
The Battle of Saratoga
The Battle of Monmouth
Slavery and Indentured Servants in the Colonies
Spanish Missions in California
Spies in the Revolutionary War
St. Augustine
The First Colleges in the United States
Thomas Paine
The Loyal Tories
Transportation in the Colonies
Unsuccessful Colonies before Jamestown
The Winter at Valley Forge
Women in the American Revolution

MP4824

LEARN MORE ABOUT EARLY AMERICA ★☆★☆★☆★☆★☆★☆☆

RESOURCES FOR STUDENTS

Abigail Adams: Witness to a Revolution by Natalie Bober

American Crafts: Easy-to-Make Projects from Traditional Folk Crafts by Madeline H. Guyon

American Revolution (Eyewitness Books) by Stuart Murray

Colonial American Craftspeople by Bernardine S. Stevens

Colonial American Home Life by John F. Warner

Colonial Crafts and Tools and Gadgets by Bobbie Kalman

Deborah Sampson: Soldier of the Revolution by Harold Felton

Eating the Plates: A Pilgrim Book of Food and Manners by Lucille Recht Penner

Founding the American Colonies by Diana Reische

George and Martha Washington at Home in New York by Beatrice Siegel

If You Lived in Colonial Times by Ann McGovern

If You Were There in 1776 by Barbara Brenner

Making Thirteen Colonies by Joy Hakim

Patriots in Petticoats by Patricia Edwards Clyne

The American Revolutionaries: A History in Their Own Words 1750–1800, edited by Milton Meltzer

The Craftsman in America by the Special Publications Division of the National Geographic Society

The First Passage: Blacks in the Americas by Colin A. Palmer

The Papermakers, The Tanners, The Weavers, and The Cabinetmakers by Leonard Fisher

The Serpent Never Sleeps by Scott O'Dell

The Story of the Bonhomme Richard by Norman Richards

The Story of the Surrender at Yorktown by Zachary Kent

The Witch of Blackbird Pond by Elizabeth George Speare

Those Remarkable Women of the Revolution by Karen Zeinert

Websites:

http://www.ic.sunysb.edu/Class/est572/joreste/
"Colonial America" Activity Ideas for Elementary School
http://www.socialstudiesforkids.com/articles/ushistory/13colonies2.htm
The Thirteen Colonies. Also has articles and links related to the Revolutionary War.
http://usparks.about.com/cs/revwarinfo/
Revolutionary War Information Sources
http://www.ushistory.org/march/
Virtual Marching Tour of the American Revolutionary War
http://www.contemplator.com/folk3/worldtur.html
The World Turned Upside Down (Words and music)

There are too many wonderful websites to mention. To find more, use such keywords as the following: *colonial activities, American Revolution, War for Independence, Revolutionary War, 13 Colonies*. Many vocabulary words and personalities presented on the activity pages also make good starting points for searches.

★☆★☆★☆★☆★☆★☆★☆★☆★☆★☆★☆★☆★☆★☆★☆★☆★☆★☆ **27**

MP4824

AN$WER KEY ★☆★☆★☆★☆★☆★☆★☆★☆★☆★☆★☆★☆★☆

The First European Settlements, page 2
1. See transparency for locations. 2. Jamestown: England,
St. Augustine: Spain, Quebec, France

English, Dutch, Swedish, Spanish and French, page 3
The Swedish were in a small section of Delaware. The
Dutch were in New York. The French were in Canada and
the Spanish were in Florida and the Southwest.

Whose Land Is This Anyway?, page 4
1. See transparency for locations. 2. Wetu were made of
bark or mats woven with cattails. The framework was
created with bent cedar poles. The Cherokee lived in round
huts made of mats laid over poles, then plastered with
mud. The Iroquois lived in longhouses. Several families
lived together.

Courage, Hope and a Very Leaky Ship, page 5
1. false; 2. true; 3. false; 4. true; 5. true; 6. true; 7. false;
8. false; 9. false; 10. false

The Importance of the Mayflower Compact, page 6
Answers will vary, but should show an understanding that
the people will get together to make the rules and agree to
obey them.

Wild Rivers, Dense Forests, and Rich Fields, page 7
See the transparency for locations. Answers for
temperatures will vary but may be approximately as
follows: Boston: 22–32 and 68–72; Philadelphia: 23–32
and 75–80; Atlanta: 30–35 and 85–100.

Different Colonies for Different Reasons, page 8
1. e; 2. c; 3. d; 4. b; 5. h; 6. i; 7. l; 8. j; 9. k; 10. m; 11. a;
12. f; 13. g; 14. See transparency.

Daily Life in the Colonies, page 9
1. a child's bed stored under the parents' bed; 2. a sleigh
pulled by two horses; 3. carrier of news; 4. a shoemaker;
5. an iron worker who made pots, nails, and horseshoes;
6. made leather for boots, buckets, and even pants;
7. a clock without a case; 8. a barrel maker; 9. made tin
items such as candleholders; 10. a mail carrier

Toad Tea and Rattlesnake Oil, page 11
1. Answers will vary, but may include: Same: tried to heal
people, used medicine, did surgery, told people to rest and
keep warm, used vaccine. Different: used bleeding,
prescribed different medicines, some were not trained in
universities, had to travel long distances, did not know
about germs; 2. prescribed powdered toads, kept warm,
used herbs; 3. doctor, surgeon, apothecary; 4. Doctors were
expensive and often lived far away; 5. there are germs
(many other possible answers); 6. cancer, AIDS etc.

How a Poet Created a Hero, page 14
2. Many possible answers, but should include the facts
that Paul Revere did not see the signal from the Old North
Church and he never made it to Concord. 4. Revere is
famous because Longfellow wrote the poem about him.
(He was also very active in Patriot organizations before
the Revolution, but that is not widely known.)

Colonial and Revolutionary Money, page 15
2. It is hard to make change if there are too few
denominations. 3. It is confusing if there are too
many denominations.

Fighting Words, page 19
1. hatchet: an ax; 2. spontoon: a pole weapon; 3. breeches:
pants; 4. musket: a gun; 5. frontier hunting shirt: a uniform
for Continentals 6. dragoon: a soldier on horseback;
7. powder horn: a container for gun powder; 8. haversack:
a solder's linen satchel; 9. cannon: a field gun; 10. fife: a
musical instrument; 11. tricorn: a hat; 12. bicorn: a hat;
13. Grenadier: a member of an elite guard; 14. indigo: a
blue dye; 15. militia: citizen soldiers; 16. ammunition:
bullets and shot; 17. infantry: foot soldiers

Some Amazing People, page 20
1. George Washington; 2. Nathan Hale; 3. Benedict Arnold;
4. Baron Von Steuben; 5. John Hancock; 6. Paul Revere;
7. Thomas Paine; 8. Patrick Henry; 9. Cornwallis;
10. Benjamin Franklin; 11. Rochambeau; 12. Lafayette

After the War (Review), page 23
1. j; 2. n; 3. l; 4. k; 5. a; 6. b; 7. c; 8. m; 9. d; 10. h;
11. e; 12. f; 13. g; 14. i

Then and Now, page 25
Many farmers grow corn: both, Children keep pets: both,
Boys become apprentices: then, People fish: both, People
enjoy singing: both, People read newspapers: both, People
travel in cars: now, Children play with toys: both, Children
go to school: both (or now) People go to inns to hear news:
then, Boys play marbles: both, People drink toad
tea to feel better: then, Most letter carriers ride on
horseback: then, Children learn to read from hornbooks:
then, People watch television: now: Other similarities:
people eat bread, they sleep in houses, they work, they
raise children, they dance, some go to church, they need
a government, there are punishments when people break
rules, they need heat in the winter, they need to keep
warm and rest when they are sick, etc. Differences: Better
medical care, better transportation, better communication,
more books, planes, trains, cars, paved highways, central
heat, air conditioning, computers etc.

 MP4824